The 5 Minute

Mindfulness P

20 Simple Habits T ... ce Anxie

The 5 Minute S ... ook 3)

Magnus Muller

Legal & Disclaimer

The information contained in this book and its contents is not designed to replace nor take the place of any form of medical or professional advice; it is not meant to replace the need for independent medical, financial, legal or other professional advice or services, as may be required. The content and information in this book has been provided for educational and entertainment purposes only.

The content and information contained in this book has been compiled from sources deemed reliable, and it is accurate to the best of the Author's knowledge, information and belief. However, the Author cannot guarantee its accuracy and validity and cannot be held liable for any errors and/or omissions. Further, changes are periodically made to this book as and when needed. Where appropriate and/or necessary, you must consult a professional (including but not limited to your doctor, attorney, financial advisor or such other professional advisor) before using any of the suggested remedies, techniques, or information in this book.

Upon using the contents and information contained in this book, you agree to hold harmless the Author from and against any damages, costs, and expenses, including any legal fees potentially resulting from the application of any of the information provided by this book. This disclaimer applies to any loss, damages or injury caused by the use and application, whether directly or indirectly, of any advice or information presented, whether for breach of contract, tort, negligence, personal injury, criminal intent, or under any other cause of action.

You agree to accept all risks of using the information presented inside this book.

You agree that by continuing to read this book, where appropriate and/or necessary, you shall consult a professional (including but not limited to your doctor, attorney, or financial advisor or such other advisor as needed) before using any of the suggested remedies, techniques, or information in this book. While the book refers to real-life situations, the names mentioned may have been changed.

The 5 Minute Self Help Series

The 5 Minute Self Help Series (Book 1)

The 5 Minute Procrastination Addiction Cure
Eliminating Procrastination By Starting In 5 Minutes Or Less

By Magnus Muller

Kindle: http://www.amazon.com/dp/B07CT215ZZ
Paperback: http://www.amazon.com/dp/1983161640

The 5 Minute Self Help Series (Book 2)

The 5 Minute To-Do List Formula
A Diagrammatic Guide To Complete Your Task Within 2 Weeks

By Magnus Muller

Kindle: http://www.amazon.com/dp/B07F8HFDLC
Paperback: http://www.amazon.com/dp/1983360260

The 5 Minute Self Help Series (Book 3)

The 5 Minute Mindfulness Practical Guide
20 Simple Habits To Lead A Stress Free Life, Reduce Anxiety And Treat Depression

By Magnus Muller

Kindle: http://www.amazon.com/dp/B07F8H6ZS2
Paperback: http://www.amazon.com/dp/1983360392

Author's message

After completing my first book, "The 5 Minute Procrastination Addiction Cure" and my second book, "The 5 Minute To Do List Formula", I have embarked on my third book, "The 5 Minute Mindfulness Practical Guide".

Mindfulness is a topic familiar to many but not everyone can master the techniques of mindfulness. This third book serves to help readers, including beginners and also those who struggle emotionally, to be able to worry less and lead a stress-free life.

In this book, I have provided 20 simple habits that you can use. Do try out all of them and pick the ones that really helps you to achieve your goals.

Enjoy your read and I hope that after reading this book, you will finally be able to reduce anxiety, eliminate depression and lead a stress-free life.

Table of Contents

Introduction

Do you know that every day we have between 50,000 to 70,000 thoughts? Of these, 90% are useless repetitive negative thoughts. With all these unhelpful thoughts going on, it is no wonder our overcrowded mind doesn't give us any chance to take a breather and truly experience life. Therefore is it any surprise that many of us struggle with anxieties, negative thinking and depression?

According to the Mental Health Of America, depression is the most common mental illness affecting more than 16 million Americans each year. Symptoms of depression include sadness, hopelessness, loss of interest in life and in extreme cases one out of every ten people commit suicide; such as what happened tragically to fashion designer Kate Spade and celebrity chef Anthony Bourdain.

So how do we keep these repetitive and negative thoughts away without resorting to anti-anxiety and antidepressant medications which normally have side effects? By applying mindfulness we can reduce the impact of anxieties on our mind and body. But what is mindfulness?

Mindfulness is not about emptying your thoughts or feelings but awakening your forgotten human ability to be fully present. Simply put, mindfulness means paying attention to the present moment instead of rushing through.

For example instead of gulping down your coffee by the sink, you intentionally take time to savor the aromatic coffee with no distractions of what you need to do next. It is about creating a space whereby you can observe your thoughts and feelings without attachment. Imagine being able to let all your negative, worry and fearful thoughts float away like a balloon, instead of hanging on to them.

In this book, you will learn how to use mindfulness to successfully quiet your mind, thus becoming more balanced and fulfilled in life. When you consistently apply the 5-minute mindfulness solutions in this book, you will set yourself free from repetitive negative thoughts dominating your life.

Chapter 1: Why most people suffer from negative thinking, anxiety and depression

The National Institute of Mental Health revealed that 40 million Americans are plagued by anxiety and depression related disorders. Statistics show that 50% of college students constantly feel overwhelmed, while adults regularly suffer from sleeplessness and poor memory. What most do not realize is these are symptoms of depression. Most people will not diagnose themselves as depressed but they'll openly admit feeling stressed, anxious, having a loss of appetite and the inability to make an effort in life.

All of us have different reaction to handling stress, depending on your upbringing and genetic makeup. Some people appear to be more resilient and view stressful situations as challenges while others who persistently hide from it can lead to depression. What we call stress is what psychologists term as anxiety which is a risk factor for depression.

Why people are suffering more

Reason 1: Fear of the unknown

Excessive worrying about the present and future is essentially a fear of the unknown. For example we worry about our children's safety at a school excursion, or we fear we'll not have enough for our retirement due to rising living costs. Every day we worry about countless things that never happen. Unfortunately this habit of worrying puts us in a constant state of stress and anxiety.

Reason 2: Unrealistic expectations and competitiveness

As our society becomes more affluent, we become more driven on material goals such as money and status. As such we often set high bars for ourselves to achieve and constantly compare ourselves to others. We want to look like Hugh Jackman and Jennifer Lawrence with the bank account of Mark Zuckerberg. Every day we are competing with 7.6 billion people all wanting to be good looking, famous and rich. As a result we're stressed out trying to impress others with our clothes, gadgets, cars and status or we become plagued by negative thinking that we'll never be on par with others. All we get in the end is a vicious cycle of unrealistic expectations and disappointments in life.

Reason 3: Rise of technology

Technology is a good thing but the problem is we're constantly bombarded with emails, texts, mobile phones, Facebook etc. which means there's always a demand to respond immediately. Have you ever been woken up in the middle of the night by your boss' text or a friend asking for help? When you're taking the subway or waiting for the bus do you notice almost everyone is looking at their phone? Instead of noticing the sights and sounds around us or even our family, we're constantly looking at a tiny screen which can lead to build up of stress and tension. Often our lives are moving so fast that our brains have no time to process all the information overload.

Reason 4: Lack of social and family support

Social interactions with friends and family can be a pillar of support and happiness. Those with weak or poor relationship and social ties are also twice more likely at risk for depression. Unfortunately modern people now spend more time at the office than at home.

You can lead a stress free and carefree life

The truth is we'll never be completely stress free because there will always be family drama, deadlines at work, financial crisis or sudden health problems. Although we can't control what happens around us, we can change how we react to stress and negative situations. We can achieve this by learning simple techniques to manage the stress triggers in our lives such as our family, job, unhealthy habits like drinking and smoking or even addictions to social media.

If you feel your life is stressful and you're constantly having negative thoughts, you're not alone and there's no reason why you can't get better. The best way to start is with simple things such as right now focusing on what you're reading. Later in this book, you'll learn some simple but effective 5-minute mindfulness solutions to help you break out of negative thinking and patterns. Once you remove what no longer serves you, you'll begin to enjoy a more stress free and carefree life.

Chapter 2: Why you are not getting the results that you want

Anxiety disorders happen when your irrational fears become persistent nervousness and worrying or negative thoughts that you cannot stop. If left untreated, it can progress into a cycle of negative thinking and feeling bad which is a catalyst for depression.

Symptoms of anxiety and depression

- Feeling tired and irritable

- Changes in eating habits e.g. overeating or loss of appetite

- Insomnia or un-restful sleep

- Difficulties in concentrating, making decisions or remembering things

- Prone to panic attacks

- Feeling of hopelessness and disinterest in life

- Slow in speech and movement

- Thoughts of hurting yourself

- Inability to relax

Typical methods for treating anxiety and depression

Anxiety and depression are two different disorders but both treatments normally involve a combination of counseling, behavioral therapy, psychotherapy and medication.

Method 1: Counseling

Counseling means having someone to talk to and can be very helpful for someone suffering from anxieties escalating into depression. Psychodynamic therapy is the most well-known whereby patients lie on the couch typically once a week to talk to the therapist. Other examples of counseling are hypnosis, attachment therapy, interpersonal therapy, psychoanalysis, individual therapy etc.

While counseling can be very effective, not all are created equal and you might not find the right therapist to connect with or their method might not work for you. Overall, finding the right one requires considerable time, effort and financial commitment, but it is very important to spend the time, and finances if required, to find someone who fits your style and personality, otherwise your therapy will not be successful.

Method 2: Cognitive Behavioral Therapy (CBT)

In cognitive behavioral therapy you're taught to recognize, control and change negative thinking patterns or obsessive thoughts that cause you anxieties and fears. For example instead of overreacting to your boss' housewarming party by feeling anxious and fearful you might not fit in, these therapies will teach you to identify, challenge and replace your negative beliefs and thoughts. Essentially the goal is to change the way you feel by changing the way you think.

CBT is an effective treatment for anxiety and depression because it helps you uncover the roots of your fears and worries instead of just treating the symptoms with medications. However these therapies vary greatly and you need to find one that suits your specific problems. The length and cost of therapies will also vary depending on your progress. The American Psychological Associated recommended at least 8 to 10 therapy sessions to see significant improvement.

Method 3: Working With Medications

Known as "happy pills" prescribed medications such as Prozac and Zoloft are mood enhancers used to treat anxiety and depression. However, these medications are not immediate and can take from a few weeks to months to become effective. Sometimes it will also take a while to find the right medicine and dosage as each individual responds differently. There're also common side effects such as sleepiness, fatigue, weight gain, nausea, headaches, dizziness, heart-rhythm irregularities, high blood pressure, drug and food interactions and sexual dysfunction. Understandably not everyone wants to be dependent on medications for life or live with the constant side effects. Moreover you're just using it to suppress your feelings instead of dealing with it yourself. Lastly, long term dependency can cause serious withdrawal symptoms when you want to wean off it.

At the end of the day, there's really no one-size-fits-all solution to your anxiety and stress because everyone has different underlying causes which is why people respond to treatments differently.

Chapter 3: 20 simple mindfulness solutions under 5 minutes

George Burns, famous American comedian who lived to 100 years old, once said: "If you ask what the single most important key to longevity is, I would have to say it is avoiding worry, stress and tension. And if you didn't ask me, I'd still have to say it."

Many of us are trapped in a fast-paced lifestyle, long working hours, chaotic family life, never-ending bills, poor eating habits and lifestyle choices which all adds to our daily stress. When all these stresses snowball into an insurmountable mountain, we become anxious and fearful with negative thoughts which leave us too paralyzed to overcome our problems. One thing for sure is our life will never be free from stress but we can learn to manage our stress and handle it in a way that helps us grow instead of being defeated.

Tim Ferriss the famous author of "The 4-Hour Workweek" interviewed 140 successful people who are the top of their fields ranging from sports to cryptocurrency, and found one surprising commonality. 90% of them do some type of mindfulness practice every day, and this includes Tim Ferris himself who meditates for 20 minutes every morning.

Instead of doing something drastic like quitting your job and leaving your family to join the monastery, we're just going to do one small thing at a time starting with where you are. Now chances are, you're used to equating your overly busyness and activities as productivity which actually leaves you no space or time to self-reflect. Therefore it's important that you do not let your mind question about the simplicity of the exercises, but to just do them and stick with those that work best for you. Remember we're just using mindfulness to train our mind's control over our emotions and decrease our reactivity so that we can create our life instead of being dragged by it. Thus it doesn't matter what the exercise requires you to do, as long as you put mindfulness into it you're using daily routines to help you build mental muscles.

20 simple hacks to design your daily routine

Statistics show that beginners who start exercising 30 minutes a day, for 5 days weekly usually do not last 2 months. Most of us start with the best intentions but unfortunately we often get caught up with life, family and work demands. 30 minutes may not seem like much, but it is challenging when you have to work overtime or when your kid falls sick. The good news is statistics have shown that beginners are much more likely to succeed and make it a habit if they start with 5 minutes a day, which is the purpose of our 5 minutes mindfulness hacks. Just as Confucius once said: "It does not matter how slow you go as long as you do not stop".

1) Mindful sitting

Find a place where you won't be disturbed and can sit comfortably for 5 minutes. Close your eyes and imagine a shaken snow globe with falling flakes which represent your random thoughts. Start counting backwards 10,9,8,7,6,5,4,3,2,1 while imagining the flakes (your thoughts) settling down. Each time a random thought appears, just say "okay, thank you" and return to your flakes settling down. If you feel like it, you can repeat "calm body, calm mind".

2) Mindful breathing

Find a quiet place to sit or lay down in a totally relaxed manner for 5 minutes. Take a deep breath through your nose for three seconds and exhale through your mouth for another three seconds. Repeat the cycle and start to free your thoughts about everything. As you breathe in and out observe your rising and falling thoughts. Every time your mind wanders, focus back on your breath and imagine the life force entering your body through each inhalation and you expelling all worries and fears you are holding on to with each exhalation. Do this exercise often and try increasing the duration from one to five minutes. Before you know it, you've started your own mindfulness practice.

3) Mindful seeing

For this simple 5-minute exercise, you only need a window with a view. Observe what you see outside the window and refrain from labeling. For example, do not label or think "tree", "car" or "bench". Instead pay attention to the surroundings such as a breeze blowing across the leaves or moving clouds in the sky. The main goal is to observe and be aware without injecting your own thoughts like an impartial judge. Each time you get distracted with thoughts, just focus on a spot or color.

4) Mindful listening

Although we've two ears and one mouth instead of one ear and two mouths, we still tend to talk more than we listen to others around us. However we can train our mind to be non-judgmental by training our ears. Start by listening to some neutral music such as classical or instrumental music or a song that you have no pre-association with, for example your ex-girlfriend has not recommended. Find a quiet place for 5 minutes and use your earphones to listen to the music while gently closing your eyes. Throughout the music, avoid forming any opinions of like or dislike. Accept the music for what it is, without judgment and listen till you're fully immersed. If you do this listening exercise often enough, you'll be surprised how much more you're picking up when you listen without interfering thoughts or judgment. You'll also start to see those negative thoughts that rise up are not yours but just passing thoughts.

5) Mindful eating

Most of us eat several times a day, therefore it's very easy to incorporate this 5 minutes exercise. The next time you sit down to eat, switch off all distractions such as TV, phone or computers. Take time to smell and see the color of your food and study its texture before eating. Savor and chew your food slowly while closing your eyes. In future, instead of rushing through your meals especially when you're dining with others, try to minimize conversation or eat alone away from your work desk once a week. As a bonus, mindful eaters are also more likely to lose or maintain their weight because they're not putting mindless calories into their bodies. You can also incorporate this mindful exercise into your daily tasks such as washing dishes, gardening or brushing teeth etc.

6) Mindful observation

For this simple exercise, you can use a leaf or anything of your choice to give your full attention to for 5 minutes. When holding the leaf in your hands, refrain from labeling instead just quietly observe its colors, size, shape, scent, patterns and texture. Every time you get distracted, focus your thoughts to the presence of the leaf you're holding.

7) Mindful thoughts

This exercise is about creating awareness of our own thoughts. Find a quiet place to sit or lie down for 5 minutes. Begin by bringing your awareness to any sensation in your body, then move on to your thoughts. As you observe your random thoughts for example "What am I having for lunch later?" refrain from labeling or judging. Instead see them as passing clouds or floating balloons that you do not hang on to. If you catch yourself hanging on to one of the "balloons" immediately let go. As you practice this exercise more often, you'll find yourself faster at catching yourself losing attention and getting back on the present.

8) Mindful walking

For this exercise wear comfortable clothes and shoes. Begin by taking a deep breath and briefly scan how your body feels. Start walking slowly making sure each foot makes full contact with the ground in a heel-to-toe rhythm. With each step be fully aware of your body's sensation of walking and breathing. Whenever you lose attention to random thoughts and feelings, just take notice without labeling and gently guide your focus back to the present walking. At the end of your 5 minutes' walk, stand still and take a deep breath while feeling the earth beneath your feet. You can gradually increase your walk to 20 minutes.

9) Mindful centering

For this exercise we'll light a candle (or you can use a fireplace) for 5 minutes. Since fire is naturally hypnotic, it can induce a state of stillness or trance making you feel relaxed and peaceful. Begin by sitting down comfortably in a dark or dimly lit room. Keep your posture upright and maintain eye level contact with the candle flame. The goal is to hold your focus on the flame before gently softening your gaze as you become entranced by the dancing flame. Let the flickering flame hypnotize you and whenever your mind wanders, redirect your focus on the flame. Eventually you'll notice your thoughts fading away as you experience only the present awareness of the flame.

Tip: To feel more relaxed you can also use a scented candle.

10) Mindful body scan

For this 5-minute exercise you can choose to sit or lie down, but sitting up is recommended if you're prone to falling asleep. Close or half-close your eyes and observe your own breathing. Now we'll begin from your head to your toes by observing all sensations in your body. For example, does any part of your body feel itchy, tightness, soreness, tingling or numbness? Are your shoulders tensed? Are you clenching your jaws subconsciously? If your mind starts wandering, just gently guide it back to the present scanning. The goal of noticing what your body is feeling real-time is to train your mind to pay attention in the present moment.

11) Mindful waiting

How often have we stood in line at the supermarket or fast food restaurant wishing that things will go faster? Oftentimes we even feel impatient at the people in front of us or anxious to rush out of there as soon as possible. The next time you're stuck in a queue, take the opportunity to connect with your breath. Tune in to your emotions - are you feeling anxious, rushed or impatient? Observe your feelings without judgment and learn to breathe into them, knowing that you're where you need to be right now at this present moment and accept the situation.

12) Mindful commute

Almost every day we commute via car, bus or subway thus making this exercise easy to incorporate daily. For example, the next time you're driving to the office purposely take a different route, turn off the car radio and for the next 5 minutes pay attention to your new surroundings by taking in the sights. The goal is to take notice and be present with your surroundings. Oftentimes we're so used to taking the same route home or to work that our brains turn into auto-pilot mode without making any real connection with the present moment. We can even walk past our neighbors or colleagues without registering them.

13) Mindful bedtime

Every night do you just jump into bed or do you take some time to wind down? For this 5 minute exercise you'll start by taking a good look at your bed. Feel its soft sheets against your skin and notice how soft or firm your mattress is against your body weight. Start appreciating your bed knowing how important a good sleep is. Be thankful, be appreciative and savor the present moment before falling asleep.

14) Mindful mind dump

Take out a pen and paper, and find a comfortable place to write uninterrupted. Set your timer for 5 minutes and use this time to write out any thoughts or feelings that come to your mind. Don't hold anything back or judge what you're writing. Simply write non-stop until 5 minutes is up. The goal of this exercise is to help you clear your mind by dumping out all your thoughts onto paper. At the end of this exercise you'll definitely feel some relief from all the pent up tension and stress.

15) Mindful doodle

Do you remember how you used to doodle on just about anything as a child? For some reason, most adults have forgotten how to draw, something that comes naturally to most kids. Perhaps you're convinced that you're no Picasso or Van Gogh but that's not the purpose here. Drawing is in fact a great tool in mindfulness as it requires one to concentrate and be totally aware of the subject he or she is drawing.

For the next 5 minutes, take out your pencil and paper and choose an object or subject to draw. It can be the mug sitting on your desk or your sleeping cat. With your eyes observe the lines, curves and shadows of your object and start drawing with your pencil. You can make your drawing as simple or detailed as you desire as this is not an art competition, but a simple mindfulness exercise to practice being in the present.

16) Mindful coffee or tea

There is an interesting form of meditation involving a tea ceremony, whereby Buddhist monks give their utmost attention to every aspect of the tea from preparation, brewing to drinking. Similarly you can practice this with your morning coffee. Observe the sounds coming from your coffee machine as it brews you an aromatic cup of coffee - how does it smell? Observe how its color changes when you add some cream or milk. Does the cup of coffee feel warm and inviting in your hands? Finally sip and savor your coffee knowing that you're in the present moment and everything else can wait.

17) Mindful 5-4-3-2-1 senses

This 5 minute mindful exercise is about noticing something with our five senses - sight, touch, sound, smell and taste. First we start with our eyes by noticing five non obvious things such as a small crack on the wall or a stain on the door. Next bring awareness to how you feel and identify four things, for example the texture of your shirt or the fabric of the chair you're sitting on. After that listen for three things you can hear in the background for example the humming of your refrigerator or a clock ticking. Now move on to two things you can smell for example the scent from your fresh laundry. Lastly one thing you can taste. This exercises is meant to bring you to a mindful state quickly by creating awareness with your five senses.

18) Mindful cleaning

Do you know cleaning house is a great way to rid yourself of stress and emotional baggage? If you're someone who dislikes housework, change your attitude by reframing this as a stress relief and self-understanding exercise. For this 5-minute exercise select something manageable such as cleaning your basin. As you clean the basin, focus on what you're doing and nothing else. Feel the soapy sponge you're using and imagine the dirt that you scrub out as your emotional baggage. As you rinse the basin clean, feel the release of all the stress you've been holding.

19) Mindful mantra

Some of us live in a perpetual state between fear and worry because we're plagued by non-serving negative thoughts. The Buddhists liken our thoughts to monkeys swinging from tree to tree with no purpose. To tame this monkey mind of ours, we'll use a mantra repeatedly to replace our thoughts for 5 minutes. A mantra can be anything that speaks to you for example "All is well", "The Universe takes care of me" or it can be a sound like "OM" or "AUM" which is commonly use at the end of yoga practice and symbolizes our state of consciousness as well as connection to the universe.

After you've chosen your mantra, sit comfortably in a quiet place but not too comfortably that you fall asleep. Set your timer, close your eyes and relax your body by releasing any tension you're holding. Start by repeating your mantra aloud for example "OM" before gradually reducing the sound till it's just in your head. During this exercise you'll be distracted by countless thoughts but that's ok. Just acknowledge them and come back to your mantra till time's up.

Stress happens whenever our minds stray to negative thoughts, fears and worries. The goal of this mantra exercise is to train ourselves to return to the present moment whenever our minds stray.

20) Mindful self-control

This last one is something you can do when you feel you've become more mindful. Mindful self-control is about allowing yourself to experience urges without reacting.

First get your favorite or forbidden treat such as a Snickers bar or marshmallows. Place the treat on the table without touching it. Start to notice how your body is reacting. Is your mouth salivating or your brain imagining how satisfying the gooey caramel chocolate will taste like? Now focus on what your body is really doing and how it is actually preparing itself for a sweet finale. Stay with those reactions and feel the desires building up in waves before they finally subside. Now how does it feel to be able to resist the craving? By not reacting, you're telling your mind and body that they do not own you. As such you can choose not to react to negative thoughts, fears and worries when they come up. Finally to end this exercise, put away the candy or give it to someone else as you don't want to ruin the bold declaration you just made.

Chapter 4: Bonus tips to cultivate mental strategies and mindful routines

You've already been shown 5-minute mindfulness hacks that you can do daily to manage your stress, anxieties and negative thinking. Knowing how to manage our stress is great, but wouldn't it be better if we can overcome it completely? Doing daily mindfulness exercises strengthens our mental muscle, but now we're going to give ourselves an extra boost to make it more long lasting in our lives.

10 simple ways to maintain mindfulness and reduce daily stress

1) Get moving

Exercise is not only good for your physical health, but also helps you relieve your build-up of stress and anxieties while releasing neurotransmitters that improve your mood. Yoga is known to reduce anxiety and teaches breathing techniques to help one relax. It is also an easy form of exercise that is suitable for most people. It really doesn't matter what you do, be it a nature walk, jogging or swimming just have fun doing it.

2) Relaxation

Relaxation methods such as deep breathing and visualization can help you clear your mind and become calmer so you can deal with stress better. To do a simple visualization just close your eyes, listen to some soothing music in the background or use earphones, and imagine yourself in a relaxed environment such as a sandy white beach.

3) Be healthier

Do you know that excessive smoking, alcohol and unhealthy foods contribute to your stress level? Do you also notice people who are stress eating tends to prefer unhealthy "comfort foods" such as ice-cream, potato chips and fast foods? Statistics show that poor eaters have twice the stress levels compared to the healthiest eaters. Simply put, eating better means you'll get less stress. Why not start by adding some fruits, nuts or vegetables daily and feel the positive difference? Your body will thank you.

4) Declutter your space

When you simplify your life, you make room for more light and growth. It is really hard to be clear headed when we're surrounded by excessive things around us. When we see a lot of visual clutter, it intrudes into our mental head space. In Chinese Fengshui it is believed that clearing out physical space brings in luck, wealth and good health. When we declutter we're also letting go of old energies such as fear, loss and pain. Learn to let go of belongings associated with unwanted memories and feelings.

Start with a room or your wardrobe and get rid of things that you don't use or need anymore. For clothes it could be those you haven't worn in a year. Bag them and donate the good ones to a charity. Now you've just simplified your life and have a nice clean room to look at. How does it feels to make such a clean decision? Don't be surprised at how empowered it makes you feel. You might even feel you're ready to move on to the next phase, perhaps it's starting the business you always dream about.

5) Minimize your finances stressors

Statistics show that 60% of Americans feel stressed about money especially during the holidays. If this is true for you then you already know finances can be a drain and major stress trigger. Perhaps it's time to simplify by spending less or downgrading to a smaller house? Be creative and have fun without spending money. You'll also realize that you don't need to buy a new toy every week to make yourself happy.

Meanwhile here's some tips to get you started:

- Create an expense spreadsheet and track all your expenses so that you know what's draining your finances, for example monthly gym membership which you've not used in a year. Set yourself a budget.

- Identify all your financial stressors and make a plan to tackle them. For example, installments for your sports car that takes up half your monthly paycheck or credit card bills you've trouble paying.

- Reduce temptation of overspending, for example cut up your credit cards if you know you've poor spending habits and already living from paycheck to paycheck.

- Ask for support or accountability with someone you trust and have good financial sense to help you out.

6) Do less

Having too many commitments on your plate means you're spreading yourself too thin. Take a look at your commitments and learn to prioritize while saying no to those that aren't beneficial. When you plan your schedule make sure you put some breaks in-between and not multi-tasks simultaneously. Focus on one task at a time and be fully present. Remember less is more not more is more.

7) Identify toxic relationships

We're talking about friends or even family members who regularly give you stress and drama expecting you to rescue them. These are the ones who after you've listened to their latest drama or helped them out, comes back to you repeatedly with new issues. If you see this as a pattern rather than a hallmark of good friendship, learn to avoid or cut them off. Otherwise they'll be adding more stress to your life. In the meantime surround yourself with positive friends who add to your life.

8) Let go of your past and grudges

We've all made mistakes in the past. So learn to let go and forgive yourself. Only then can you move forward in life. In the same way, if someone has wronged you, it's time to let go of your anger and grudges. If you've been walking in someone's shoes and not your own, it's time to focus on yourself and enter a new chapter.

9) Reconnect with a hobby

Was there something you used to be passionate about? Perhaps you love photography or playing the guitar? You might have put it off for years because of work or you simply lost interest in doing anything. Whatever it was, reconnect with it again and see if it still ignites your passion. If not, do something you've always wanted to try such as film making or stage acting. A hobby will not only boost your mood but also reduce your stress.

10) Gratitude log

Gratitude is one of the best cures to our negative thinking and emotions. To reap this wonderful benefit, get yourself a notebook and write down what you're thankful for during the day. You can write three to five things you're thankful for or just write non-stop for 5 minutes. The benefits are:

- Clearing of negative thoughts and emotions

- Helps create more self-awareness

- Gain new perspective from your observations

- Helps lower stress

- Something to lift you up on those days you feel a little down

Chapter 5: Benefits of mindfulness on your health and emotions

The practice of mindfulness has been around for thousands of years, but today in our busy and impulse-driven modern world, mindfulness is no longer a nice-to-have but a must-have skill in order for us to thrive.

Mindfulness based cognitive therapy (MBCT) has successfully helped people suffering from depression to deal with their negative thoughts, beliefs and feelings by recognizing what's happening and to respond instead of react. Such therapy takes as long as eight weeks to complete which is not practical for many due to time and financial constraints. However, research has found that even short mindfulness practice like the ones in this book can have tremendous benefits to us.

Benefits of mindfulness based on science

If you're still doubtful, here are some science-backed benefits of a regular mindfulness practice.

Health benefits:

1) Gray matter

The reason we become forgetful as we grow older is because our brains shrink. The good news is researchers have found that regular mindfulness practice can help increase gray matter in our brains which means it also helps us:

- Reverse age-related effects on our brains

- Improve focus in our life

- Enhance our memory

- Helps stabilize our moods and emotions

- Promotes better executive decisions

2) Amygdala

Amygdala is a section of our brain that is responsible for our fight or flight response. This is whenever you feel anxious, fearful or stressed out. For example you were driving and you just narrowly avoided hitting a kid that suddenly dashed across a dimly lit street. Your heart is still pounding and you're now perspiring profusely and breathing rapidly from the encounter. This is our amygdala at work. It aids in signaling and preparing us for dangers, and was especially useful during our ancestors' time when they had to run away from man-eating beasts. The problem is in the modern world, we're seldom in a life or death situation but our amygdala does not know the difference between real and fake dangers. When we're continuously operating in this fight or flight state, it elevates our cortisol level which increases our stress level resulting in the following:

- Anxieties, panic, jitters or paranoia

- Gloominess caused by suppressed serotonin production

- Inability to relax which can lead to sleeplessness at night

- Carbohydrate cravings causing you to eat more unhealthy food and gain weight

- Suppressed immunity causing you to fall sick more easily

- Reduced libido leading to a drop in sex drive

The good news is a research done by the University of Massachusetts and Harvard Medical School discovered that with just regular mindfulness practice they found:

- The size of the amygdala decreases meaning reduced fear, anger and stress

- Less reactivity to situations

- Lower stress and cortisol levels

- An increase in our hippocampus (gray matter) meaning better learning and memory performance

3) Beta waves

Beta waves, known as fast brain waves, are in-charge of our daily conscious tasks e.g. thinking, reading, writing, and communicating. Using MRI scans scientists show that when in over-drive our brains experience anxiety, stress and the inability to relax. However, with regular mindfulness practice we can stabilize our beta waves thus helping us to:

- Focus more

- Reduce anxiety

- Reduce stress

- Strengthen memory

- Improve problem-solving ability

- Enhance creativity

4) Serotonin

Also known as the "happy chemical" serotonin is manufactured in our brain and is a neurotransmitter that contributes to our happiness and wellbeing. When our serotonin level is up it helps:

- Lower anxiety

- Regulate our moods and emotions

- Promote mental sharpness

- Promotes restful sleep

If our serotonin levels are low it is known to cause:

- Depression

- Anxiety

- Low self-esteem

- Low mood

- Poor memory

- Insomnia

- Aggression

So how can we up our serotonin levels? Research has shown that mindfulness practice can effectively help our body to release serotonin naturally without the harmful side-effects of anti-depressant drugs such as Prozac or Zoloft which are used to increase serotonin levels in depressed patients.

5) Other health benefits

- Increase our immunity thus preventing illnesses, inflammation and infections

- Helps lower blood pressure and regulate those with symptoms of high blood pressure

- Lower heart risk, heart attack, stroke and early death.

- Helps prevent asthma, rheumatoid arthritis, inflammatory bowel disease, Alzheimer disease, fibromyalgia, psoriasis, ADHD, epilepsy etc.

Emotional benefits:

- Lower stress, worry, anxiety, fear, loneliness, depression, and impulsivity

- Improve mood and calmness

- Increase optimism, awareness and relaxation

- Promotes self-esteem and self-acceptance

- Improve one's resilience against pain and adversity

- Reduce emotional eating and other bad habits

- Improve and build positive social connections

Aren't you glad science has proven that regular mindfulness practice can really bring us health and emotional benefits? With so many amazing benefits and positive payoffs, there's no reason for you not to try any of these 5-minute mindfulness exercises which are all designed to fit into your busy lifestyle.

The take home message here is that in order to gain optimum benefits, one has to maintain a regular mindfulness practice. Nearly all the research above has shown that the key to reaping maximum results lies in consistent mindfulness practice. Remember even with 5 minutes of regular mindfulness practice, you'll also be reaping amazing health benefits for yourself in the long-term.

Tips on being consistent and maximizing your mindfulness practice

1. Identify your intention and motivation for practicing mindfulness

Is it because you're trying to break out of your negative thinking? Do you carry a lot of unfounded fears and worries that interfere with your daily life? Every time you give an excuse or don't feel like doing your mindfulness practice, remind yourself why you're doing it in the first place.

2. **Set the right attitude and intention**

Every time you sit down to do your mindfulness practice, set the right attitude and intention. Tell yourself there's no "good" or "bad" practice but you're just here to cultivate mindfulness. Understand that it is a process and cannot be rushed as you're releasing all the pent up stress and emotions. Every effort you make to be in the present is not wasted because once your mind can be relatively still, you'll experience peace and calmness from within. Just this alone will make you motivated to stay with your practice.

3. **Start small**

Don't be too ambitious by jumping to 30 minutes. The advantage with starting small like 5 minutes a day means you're less likely to miss a practice. This positive feeling of success will motivate you to be consistent in your practice. Eventually when you're ready you can slowly extend to 10, 20 or 30 minutes.

4. **Set a regular time and place**

One trick for being consistent is to set a regular time and place for your practice. For example if you set your practice at 7am every morning, you're telling your brain that this is non-negotiable and it will stop questioning or give you excuses. Once you enter into the room you designated for your practice, your mind will see the cue and auto pilot into practice mode.

5. **Find the right posture**

You don't have to sit in a lotus position if it's uncomfortable for you. Instead find your own comfortable position but preferably not so comfortable that you fall asleep during practice. It can be your favorite office chair or a cushion on the floor.

6. Lastly.... just do it!

Conclusion

Thank you for reading this book. By now you've probably gleaned enough key information on the practice of mindfulness to know that it's not a hype but a necessity in our fast-paced society.

Hopefully by now you're quite fired up to start on your mindfulness practice, but I'd like to add a gentle reminder that the real key to making your mindfulness practice work is consistency. Therefore it is more powerful and optimal for you to practice 5 minutes a day than to practice for an hour once a week or when you feel like it. With daily practice, you'll start to see your mind clearing and negative thoughts, anxieties and stress that once plagued you will roll off like "water off a duck's back".

With so many amazing benefits to practicing mindfulness, why not discover these for yourself by doing just one 5-minute exercise today? This book is of little value if you do not try these exercises yourself.

Lastly, I would like to leave you with this final quote by Kelsang Gyatso: "The purpose of mindfulness is to make our mind calm and peaceful. If our mind is peaceful, we will be free from worries and mental discomfort, and so we will experience true happiness. But if our mind is not peaceful, we will find it very difficult to be happy, even if we are living in the best conditions"

— Magnus Muller

About the author

Magnus Muller is a young writer who likes to explore the world as well as to play sports. He strongly believes that success can be attained with consistent hard work and effort.

He began writing his first book: **"The 5 Minute Procrastination Addiction Cure"**, to help those who suffer from procrastination to overcome it by just using a simple rule of thumb. He has now also published his second and third book: **"The 5 Minute To-Do List Formula"** and **"The 5 Minute Mindfulness Practical Guide"** to help his readers achieve their goals.

These 3 books come together to form **"The 5 Minute Self Help Series"**. Since these 3 books are of different topics, hence you do not need to read them in chronological order but start with any book of your choice.

To find out more about his work, check out his books at **https://amazon.com/author/magnusmuller** and you will start to enjoy more free time and accomplish your tasks!

Leave a review

If you truly enjoy this book, please help to leave a review on Amazon! This book is now available in both the kindle and paperback version.

Kindle: https://www.amazon.com/dp/B07F8H6ZS2
Paperback: https://www.amazon.com/dp/1983360392
Author: https://amazon.com/author/magnusmuller

The 5 Minute Self Help Series

The 5 Minute Self Help Series (Book 1)

The 5 Minute Procrastination Addiction Cure
Eliminating Procrastination By Starting In 5 Minutes Or Less

By Magnus Muller

Kindle: http://www.amazon.com/dp/B07CT215ZZ
Paperback: http://www.amazon.com/dp/1983161640

The 5 Minute Self Help Series (Book 2)

The 5 Minute To-Do List Formula
A Diagrammatic Guide To Complete Your Task Within 2 Weeks

By Magnus Muller

Kindle: http://www.amazon.com/dp/B07F8HFDLC
Paperback: http://www.amazon.com/dp/1983360260

The 5 Minute Self Help Series (Book 3)

The 5 Minute Mindfulness Practical Guide
20 Simple Habits To Lead A Stress Free Life, Reduce Anxiety And Treat Depression

By Magnus Muller

Kindle: http://www.amazon.com/dp/B07F8H6ZS2
Paperback: http://www.amazon.com/dp/1983360392

Check out other books

5 Steps Self Discipline Blueprint
Resist Temptations, Get Things Done and Lead the Live You Desire

By Trevor Henry

Kindle: https://www.amazon.com/dp/B07FLWHM3D
Paperback: https://www.amazon.com/dp/171778903X

33382112R00044

Printed in Great Britain
by Amazon